THE WAY WE LIVE
in the city

14/3 大众百通
01139
贰
元

上海公交汽电车乘车

1	11	21
2	12	22
3	13	23
4	14	24
5	15	25
6	16	26
7	17	27
8	18	28

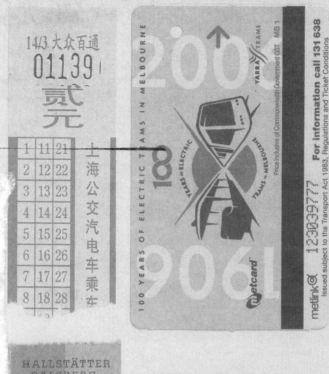

200 1906

100 YEARS OF ELECTRIC TRAMS IN MELBOURNE

YARRA TRAMS   MB 1

100 YEARS OF ELECTRIC
TRAMS IN MELBOURNE

metcard

metlink

For information call 131 638

Price inclusive of Commonwealth Government GST

123039777

Issued subject to the Transport Act 1983, Regulations and Ticket Conditions

045S003   0327312
2006/07/27
11:33

ida e volta
urbano
1,30 euros

Metropolitano de Lisboa E.P.
Cont n° 500 192 853
Preço incluindo IVA à taxa legal

99
*100
101
102

metro

Nachdruck verboten

HALLSTÄTTER
SALZBERG-
SEILBAHN

271920

Tarif E

Berg-   Tal-
Fahrt

DRUCK ZAWADIL WIEN

| 24 | 23 | 22 | 21 | 20 | 19 | 18 | 17 |
| 32 | 31 | 30 | 29 | 28 | 27 | 26 | 25 |

C.F.L.

CONSERVE-SE ESTE BILHETE

2$50 N⁰

INCLUINDO O IMPOSTO DE SELO

| 16 | 15 | 14 | 13 | 12 | 11 | 10 | 9 |
| 8 | 7 | 6 | 5 | 4 | 3 | 2 | 1 |

800692

S10/01   000495
25 Jul 2006   11:54

carris

N. Contr : 500595313

Tarifa Bordo
1,20€

CONSERVAR ATÉ AO
FIM DE VALIDADE

18. -7. -7

東京

(東京地下鉄)

東京▸160 円

小児   80円

7 5 8 3

10

発売日即日限り有効
下車前途無効

BRISTOL OMNIBUS CO. LTD.

BOING
U 07088

NOT TRANSFERABLE
Subject to Company Regulations

PENCE
SHILLINGS

Qk 3539

7	15	13
6	SEN	12
	NAIK	11
4		
3		
2		

Perkhidmatan

013002677X

10-Trip

Off-Peak
$80.75

GCT

CLD SPG

1
7

Subject to tariff regulations

Metro-North Railroad   10/17/05

B00324901

	O	O	O	O	O
		7		9	10
I	I	I	I	I	I

Bus Pass

No photocard required except
for children aged 14 and 15
and New Deal participants

Class
Ticket type   Zones   Price

BUS PASS STD

1DAY   BUS PASS

£3.50 M

Start date   24 JUN06

Expiry date   24 JUN06

Status

Issue date   24JUN06 1821

Number   UX638814 08154 24JUN06 1821

Not for resale

London Transport Issued subject to conditions – see over

STAFFORD CLIFF

THE WAY WE LIVE

in the city

WITH COLOUR PHOTOGRAPHS BY

GILLES DE CHABANEIX

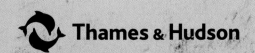
Thames & Hudson

A townhouse door (*p.1*) and apartment stairwells (*pp.2–7*) symbolize two aspects of inner-city dwelling.

THE WAY WE LIVE
in the city

Introduction 8

1
CITY HOMES
Houses, Apartments, Lofts, Conversions 16

2
CITY SPACES
Rooms, Views, Lifestyles 58

3
CITY SURFACES
Colours, Textures, Materials, Finishes 134

4
CITY DETAIL
Display, Storage, Objects, Art 166

5
CITY LIFE
Streets, Squares, Food Markets, Flea Markets 224

Index 254
Acknowledgments 256

INTRODUCTION

The city, especially the inner city – that intense concentration of humanity and construction – has enjoyed something of a renaissance during the last twenty years. Rather than fleeing to the leafy suburbs or even country towns and villages, style-conscious people have been gradually resettling the city centre. Former warehouses, light industrial premises and workshops are being transformed by designers, architects and perceptive home-owners into lofts and apartments of all shapes and sizes, packed with clever design and decoration solutions, and frequently state-of-the-art technology. Even in Paris and New York, cities which have always had vibrant downtown communities and cultures, buildings that once housed factories, markets and offices are now available as the new material for domestic conversion, while the original businesses move to out-of-town locations.

Such developments, strongly reflected in the pages which follow, are especially noticeable in the nineteenth-century cities of Europe and North America, where the most concentrated urban areas have been given new vitality, where new types of living space can become ingenious expressions of personality and individual taste. And along with this sense of revival comes the renewal of activity in public places, an intensification of street-life: in street cafés, in bars, restaurants, shops and galleries. It is this new sense of vibrancy in the city which is the focus of this book.

This is also a book about differences, about how the architecture and topographies of various cities have an effect upon the habits of their inhabitants and on the

definition of their homes. These differences make for the charm, energy and attraction of places as diverse as London, Paris, New York, Los Angeles, Istanbul, Sydney and Tokyo.

Let us imagine, for instance, a visit to a young couple living in a *fin-de-siècle* apartment building in the rue Jacob in the 6th *arrondissement* of Paris. First, you'll need the code to punch into the panel beside the fortress-like wooden front doors which give on to the street. Once inside, you will almost certainly be confronted by a courtyard, a secluded area remote from the noise and bustle of the street only a few feet away. Then you will face a number of other choices – several doorways or perhaps well-worn stone steps – or a rattling old lift with doors you open and close yourself, and for the entrance to which you will almost certainly need another set of code numbers. Once upstairs, there will be a bell or a door-knocker to be negotiated before you finally make your entrance into the apartment – and another world. If the owners are a young couple, designers maybe – or in marketing or the fashion business – you may very well discover a space in sharp contrast to the gloomy atmosphere of the old building. The apartment will be bright, sun-filled and shockingly modern in its furnishings – even if the moulded ceilings, panelled walls and traditional fireplaces of the rooms have been retained. There might even be a tiny balcony with a view of the famous Paris rooftops, of the Seine, or other iconic landmarks of the city.

Visiting somebody in a house in Tokyo or Kyoto, on the other hand, couldn't be more different. For a start, you will need them to write down their address and telephone number in Japanese, so that you can show it to your taxi-driver who,

Sometimes one has a sense that the high-rises of Manhattan – here seen prior to the attacks of 9/11 (*overleaf*) – and the Hong Kong waterfront (*pp.14–15*) have become strangely divorced from the land on which they stand, the latter compressed out of existence by the overwhelming weight of the masonry above.

once he is close to the house, will call the occupants to obtain more precise directions. House numbers do not begin at one end of a street and continue to the other, but proceed erratically, following the order in which the houses were built.

Other cities, other ways: thoroughfares in Los Angeles, for instance, may extend for as much as twenty miles, so cross-street referencing is essential, as indeed it is for New York and a number of other North American cities. London, meanwhile, presents a very different vision of the city, being essentially a network of joined-up villages, retaining many of their original characteristics in an odd mixture of shops and pubs, townhouses and flats. Visiting somebody here will almost certainly entail negotiating the London Underground system, or hailing a reliable black cab.

It is such urban diversity that forms a considerable part of the photographic work of Gilles de Chabaneix: cities viewed as complete entities, evidenced in his dramatic 'overview' pictures, as well as cities in close-up: the pattern and texture of everyday things – streets and squares, markets, bars, cafés and people. The latter, the inhabitants who create the special atmosphere of cities, figure prominently in the pages which follow, represented in the individual rooms which demonstrate their creativity, glimpsed at bar counters, on restaurant terraces, bargaining in flea markets, or simply hanging out on the street. In all respects, then, this book is about the experience of being 'urbane' – a celebration of city life.

CHAPTER 1

CITY HOMES

Houses, Apartments, Lofts, Conversions

Although some of the examples of urban lifestyles, both exterior and interior, on the pages which follow have similarities, as people respond to the intensities and pressures of city living, there are also many differences in the form and shape of cities, as well as in their interiors. Some, like Paris and New York, are largely cities of apartments; indeed, the loft – converted from industrial space – came to characterize the latter, rather than the brownstone townhouse of the nineteenth-century city. In contrast, Los Angeles is a city of sprawling suburban housing. London has traditionally been a city of houses and gardens, a reflection of the English practice of bringing the countryside into the town, although conversions to apartments in the inner city have changed its character. But wherever they are, all the exteriors and interiors illustrated here are fascinating and frequently enticing as solutions to living and working in the city.

Business skyscrapers and residential blocks mix in the urban intensity of New York's Manhattan (*these pages*).

Los Angeles (*overleaf*) conforms to a very different model of American city: centres of high-rise commercial building linked by expressways to low-density habitation.

Most major cities can be symbolized by an iconic structure; in these images (*left* and *opposite*) the Eiffel Tower appears as a replica in a Paris apartment, while the real thing is just visible from a loft dwelling in the same city, beyond its famous rooftops. Another powerful icon of sophisticated urban living emphatically occupies the foreground: the 'Barcelona' chair, designed by Mies van der Rohe for the German pavilion at the Barcelona exhibition of 1929.

The city framed and, to a certain extent, brought inside to decorative effect; both these views, from a Brussels loft (*above*) and a San Francisco apartment (*right*) use the view of the city outside as a kind of 'captured' tableau, emphasizing their own role as small oases right in the centre of urban intensity. Any rectilinearity in the Brussels space is broken by the circular device, while the understated décor of the view over San Francisco makes a special feature of the windows as focal points, dominating an interior which has been stripped of all traditional features.

Rooms with a view, but very different views and very different versions of the city: cool, classical elegance is framed by a St. Petersburg balcony (*above*); a multi-lane highway forms a moving background to this Tokyo apartment (*right*).

The 'faces' of cities, their individual looks, are derived from the façades along their streets. And within the façades, the shape of windows and their surrounds plays a uniquely important role in defining that look, from *fin-de-siècle* Barcelona, to gothic Venice, to the sober gables of Amsterdam (*opposite*).

BRUSSELS

BRUSSELS

BRUSSELS

BRUSSELS

VENICE

BRUSSELS

BRUSSELS

BRUSSELS

BOMBAY

ISTANBUL

LONDON

BARCELONA

NEW YORK

City buildings are often expressive of the dominant characteristics of the cultures which built them. Contrast, for instance, the urbane elegance of Georgian London with the gritty, no-nonsense style of the turn-of-the-century New York apartment block. And the whole might of nineteenth-century Russia is forcefully rendered in the sweeping façades of the St. Petersburg palaces (*opposite*).

On the inside looking out – in this case, to the formal vistas of the gardens of the Palais Royal, Paris (*opposite*) – windows can be major features in the city interior (*right*) as well as in the external architecture. They allow the cityscape into urban living and working spaces. They may be embellished by curtains or blinds and shutters, partly veiled or open to reveal some city vista, or provide the ideal position for a favourite chair (*overleaf*).

PARIS

PARIS

PARIS

LONDON

NAPLES

PARIS

LOS ANGELES

ISTANBUL

PARIS

The conversion of former industrial premises into urban accommodation, originally much associated with developments in 'sixties and 'seventies New York, has become a common enough phenomenon in all major cities. Heavily upholstered traditional furniture makes a strong decorative point when placed with the stark surroundings of the original windows and large, open spaces in this New York apartment (*opposite*). 'Rooms' are created more by the grouping of furniture than by the position of intersecting walls. Converted from a former print workshop, this example in Paris (*right*) retains a contact with its industrial past in the tubular stair-rails and metal storage units.

A very 'city' look for kitchen and dining areas: both these examples (*above* and *opposite*) are in Paris apartments. Where space is at a premium and needs to be carefully managed, great attention has been paid to the way the various elements – fixed units and movable furniture – relate to each other. Storage is neat and practical, yet manages to be decoratively pleasing; dining tables can double as work surfaces.

Clarity in all forms was obviously the guiding principle behind the decoration of this New York apartment (*opposite*). The pale colours of the walls and the wooden flooring make the most of the light flooding in through the large window. There are relatively few articles of furniture, but some brilliant splashes of colour provide visual drama.

As major cities have benefited from the revival of their central areas, so too space and light have acquired a rarity value in the contemporary urban environment. The pursuit of both is what matters in the lifestyle decisions made by many people. One solution is to search out larger properties originally intended for non-residential purposes – warehouses and industrial premises, for instance – and to transform them into personalized space, like this Paris loft (*right*), left comparatively untreated.

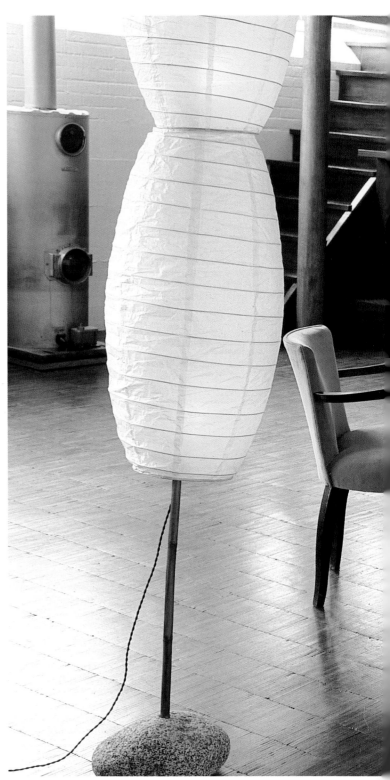

The interiors of a group of lofts near Paris, now occupied by a colony of artists, are particularly interesting for their combination of disparate objects and furniture in what was originally a semi-industrial environment. This arrangement (*above* and *right*) has something of an installation air about it: an industrial stove, traditional furniture, modern bar stools, a Japanese paper lamp and filing cabinets are, at first sight, unlikely companions. Extra space is created by the gallery.

The spaciousness of loft living also acts as inspiration for other houses and apartments, notable in this Paris example (*left*) in the use of interpenetrating spaces and extended white wall surfaces. In this case, too, the varying floor and wall areas provide ideal display spaces for the owner's personal collections.

The arrangement of floors around a central well in the same apartment allows light to flood through from space to space (*right* and *overleaf*). The exposed columns and floorboards suggest the basic structure of the building. There is a similarly spacious feeling about this Paris apartment (*pp.46–47*), accentuated by the monochromatic colour scheme – an appropriate setting for the owner's collection of iconic photographic images of Picasso.

Nineteen-fifties style is clearly a dominant theme in this Los Angeles apartment (*pp.48–49*). The stripping back of the upper wall and exposure of the ceiling joists contrast dramatically with the heavy padding of the furniture.

The following pages illustrate two very different ways of treating the classic interiors of large Paris apartments. One example (*pp.50–51*) is characterized by an engaging eclecticism in its arrangement of art objects and 'thirties style furniture. The second (*pp.52–53*), in contrast, has sought an overall harmony in the arrangement of furnishings, objects and paintings, entirely in keeping with the general Empire-style look of the space.

In strict contrast, although with an elegant modernist classicism all of its own, is this apartment (*pp.54–55*): an arrangement of essentially formal shapes, whose simplicity is thrown into relief by the exposed boards of the floor.

More immediately homely is the New York apartment (*pp.56–57*), decorated and furnished in what might be described as New England country style. The model church recalls exactly the village architecture of the north-eastern United States. Other touches include the use of traditional textiles and the presence of rustic furniture.

CHAPTER 2
CITY SPACES
Rooms, Views, Lifestyles

Behind the façades of houses or apartment blocks, beyond the squares and thoroughfares, lie the intimate spaces of city life. These are shaped in different ways in different cities. Kitchens and bathrooms, for instance, need special care in space management in 'apartment' cities. 'House' cities, such as Los Angeles and London, can afford to be more generous. The styles of the rooms illustrated in the pages which follow vary considerably, but they have all been chosen because they represent a positive response to the pressures of the urban environment. Some seem deliberately to embrace the grittiness and hardness of the city: minimalist décor; the use of hyper-functional furniture and components. Others reply to the tempo of the conurbation by seeking a softer, distinctly homely look.

Each city has its unique, individual way of shaping the living spaces of its inhabitants – a mixture of history, necessity and accident. Here we look at the complex rooftops of Prague.

The development of the townhouse was one elegant solution to the problems of living with a reasonable level of dignity and privacy in a large conurbation. And many a major city developed its own individual version of the basic unit. The row houses of Sydney (*left above*) are distinguished by their wealth of cast iron decoration, especially on their first-floor balconies. San Francisco's villas (*left below*), familiarly known as 'painted ladies', provide a vision of the domestic in the midst of the high-rise city.

The townhouses of England and the Netherlands are close cousins: a narrow entrance hall gives on to a staircase with landings, from which the rooms lead off, diminishing in size as the upper floors are reached. Such spaces are the common living experience of the city-dwellers of Amsterdam (*right above*) and of London (*right below*). However, the pressure of demand for urban accommodation has led to the conversion of many such houses into separate apartments.

The island unit and the no-nonsense cooker and other fittings give out a strong feel of 'city' in this Paris scene. A dramatic backdrop to culinary activity is provided by the famous rooftops, an indication of how intense and concentrated life is in the city. The two walls of glass are screened at night by rattan blinds.

Two strictly working kitchens in Paris apartments; one example (*left above* and *opposite*) has recycled a carpenter's work-bench to achieve an island unit. The other example (*left below*) uses semi-industrial units for storage, but still manages to create a lived-in effect by the accumulation of crockery and utensils; the 'Tizio' lamp adds an elegant note.

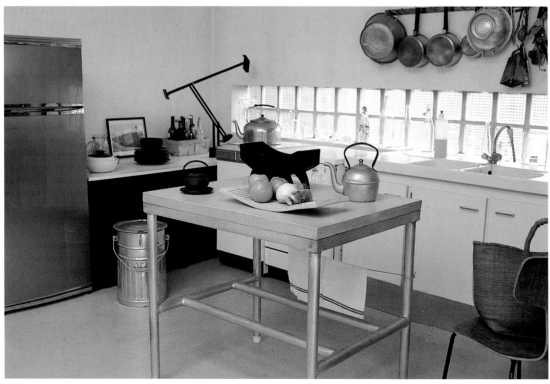

Supremely functional, but with quirky decorative touches, this kitchen-cum-dining area fits neatly into a converted roof cavity (*right*). The demands on space of modern urban life often serve to re-emphasize the central role of the kitchen in our culture; this is the room where many of us choose to eat, entertain and relax, and where food can be served directly from its place of preparation.

Finding ways of linking kitchen areas with other parts of a house often calls for considerable design ingenuity. In this interior of a house in Marseilles, great care has been taken to minimize the visibility of the actual culinary equipment. The extractor unit above the cooking surface (*left*) appears shielded and disguised, when viewed from the dining area (*opposite*). Beneath it, the main kitchen unit looks almost like a conventional living-room cabinet.

Another approach to the city cooking/dining area is the 'happening' kitchen, in which the room normally associated with food preparation extends the decorative possibilities of a house or apartment. In these four examples, cooking utensils are mingled with more formal displays on open shelves. These are kitchens to be lived in, centres of their own dwellings, places of warmth and comfort, where objects of interesting forms and colours but of no particular value can add another dimension to the purely utilitarian aspect.

In contrast to the eclectic clutter of the city kitchens illustrated on the foregoing pages, these two examples in Los Angeles have an uncompromisingly modernist and utilitarian air. Streamlined forms and cool colours characterize the one (*left*), while the other (*opposite*) is dominated by the cooker and its associated utensils. Both kitchens employ island units; these can serve both as extensions of the work surface and as dining spaces.

A suitably eclectic array of objects in
the kitchen of an old London house
(*above*) looks like an extension of the
owner's trade in antiques. The rustic
furniture and arrangement of pots
and wooden bowls are dominated by
a wood-burning Aga stove.

This kitchen installation in a Paris apartment (*above*) is clearly a place devoted to serious food preparation. However, certain decorative touches, like the display of canisters and jugs in front of the window, contribute to a lived-in effect.

Boldness in the choice of either decorative colours or forms is the keynote of the three kitchens illustrated on these pages. A massive, almost industrial cooker dominates the kitchen in a Milan apartment (*above left*). Decorative floor and wall tiles make strong patterns in another Parisian dwelling (*above right* and *opposite left*); even the cooker's ventilation unit has provided more surfaces for decoration. In an old London townhouse (*see p.74*) extensive use has been made of fixtures and utensils recycled from a bygone age (*opposite right*); what was simple and basic has here become chic and sophisticated.

In a Milan apartment (*left*) the traditional sink has received an elegant, and expensive, update in white marble. Once again, utensils are mixed with pure ornament in a fascinating visual display. A fabric curtain conceals the shelves below the sink.

Kitchens, often full of interesting shapes and intriguing objects, present constant opportunities for display, and usually look the better for it when this is done with a sensitive regard for colour and form (*right*). Crockery can look wonderful on open shelves, combined with utensils from the pre-plastics age (*opposite*).

Two West Coast examples of how city kitchens can be enlivened by the open display of objects and utensils, in Los Angeles (*above*) and in San Francisco (*opposite*): specific areas like dressers, work surfaces and shelves invite special attention.

Displays, as here, can combine the normal accoutrements of food preparation with ornaments and wall decoration, even a table lamp, into an overall, integrated design.

Space is often at a premium in the city kitchen, but even the smallest spaces can be transformed into pleasant environments by the intelligent use of available storage and display space and the visually effective disposition of crockery and utensils. All these examples, albeit in very different places, have a compactness and a neatness in common: Paris (*above left*); Istanbul (*above right*); Saigon (*opposite left*); and New York (*opposite right*).

Modernist kitchens sometimes have a distinctly industrial look; in the case of these two neatly installed cooking areas (*left* and *opposite*), however, their appearance is entirely appropriate in that they are both located in New York lofts converted from former commercial buildings. Any spartan element in the appearance of the units is countered by the displays of stylish kitchen utensils and ingredient containers. The use of industrial shelving units (*opposite*) recalls the High-Tech style of the 1970s, characterized by the use of heavy-duty industrial artefacts and equipment in domestic contexts.

Lit by the light from the traditional bay window of a London Victorian terrace house, this cool, minimalist dining area looks distinctly Oriental in inspiration (*opposite*). The rectilinear design starts at floor level in the form of wide boards of Oregon pine. The decorative devices of the original Victorian house have gone and the interior walls removed. All clutter is stored in floor-to-ceiling cupboards which run the length of one wall. A very different approach to furnishing a dining area is taken by this vaguely rustic setting (*above left*) in San Francisco (*see p.83*), while elegance is the keynote for this Paris apartment (*above right*). The dining table is in fact a conversion from a traditional Indian day-bed.

There is a spare elegance about all the dining areas illustrated on these pages, a careful regard for style which transcends national and cultural differences, for these examples do indeed come from very different cities: San Francisco (*above left*); London (*above right*); New York (*opposite left*); and Los Angeles (*opposite right*). None of the windows or tables have any form of cover, while the walls are pretty well devoid of colour and pattern.

The quietly understated modernism of this Paris apartment (*see pp.54-55*) is extended to the dining area by means of interlocking spaces (*above* and *right*). Eating thus becomes associated with the more relaxed social activity of the sitting area. The upholstered dining chairs match those in the living area, as does the woodwork. A mirror set into the alcove gives the illusion of open flow from one space to the other.

This San Francisco apartment (*above*) also makes use of connecting devices, like the large open door arch, to bring the dining-room into contact with other areas on the same floor. The whole arrangement is entirely contemporary yet, at the same time, utterly classical.

In contrast, a Paris kitchen and
dining area (*above*) makes a virtue
out of eclecticism. High-Tech style
office chairs are dramatically
juxtaposed with a dining table
created out of an antique Indian bed.

There is something about long tables
which suggests generosity and the
possibility of long, leisurely lunches,
especially when their setting is
bordering on the alfresco, as in this
Los Angeles house (*above*). More
enclosed, but equally tempting as a
setting for gastronomic delight, is
this kitchen in a Neapolitan house
(*opposite*).

A well-stocked library or book-room
should grace every thinking person's
house or apartment, the repository
of the intellectual proclivities of
the owners. By setting some of the
bookcases at an angle, the designer
of the interior (*right*) has introduced
an interesting visual conceit into a
room made even more sumptuous
by its distinctive Art Deco furniture.
The table suggests use as a dining
area or as reading room.

The dining-room in the home of a distinguished Parisian furniture designer is enlivened by the extraordinary forms of his signature chairs. Their distinguishing characteristic is the 'rope' effect applied to their backs and lower parts (*left*).

Opening to the outside, yet still part of the house, this *fin-de-siècle* Paris conservatory – retaining its magnificent ceiling and original light fitting – provides plenty of space for elegant dining (*right*). The opulence of its construction makes it the perfect setting for stylish eating.

These two Paris interiors – both obviously dining areas (*left* and *opposite*) – have an engaging eccentricity and a sense of comfort, built up by a concentration of pattern, texture, small objects and furniture. In the one (*left*), everything is arranged ship-shape fashion, as befitting a house-boat on the Seine; the other (*right*) makes an impression by the intensity of visual and ornamental elements, coupled with the quirkiness of the furniture.

If the two principles of interior decoration could be categorized as, first, a striving after pure, unadorned line and form, and second, as a glorying in elaboration and decoration, there would be no doubt where the sympathies of the owners of these two apartments would lie. Both arrangements achieve a dramatic effect by the accumulation of furniture, objects and visual decoration – the one creating an environment of colourful comfort (*above*), the other developing an overall gothic theme (*opposite*).

The successful management of space is often the key to making the most of city living, especially within the restricted confines of small apartments; in this, the ingenious and dramatic use of adjoining spaces characteristic of Japanese minimalism has much to teach us. Flexibility in defining living areas is achieved by the use of lightweight sliding screens, both wooden (*fusuma*) and in paper over a light frame (*shoji*), allowing 'rooms' to be open or closed as required: in a Kyoto house (*above*) and, most interestingly, in a Paris apartment (*opposite*).

Simple yet stylish city bedrooms, in Los Angeles (*opposite*) and Paris (*above*); in all these cases, an evident taste for gracious living has been satisfied by meticulous attention to decorative detail, using only one or two carefully chosen pieces of furniture. The use of white fabrics, especially, gives each room a 'soft' quality, creating retreats from the harsher demands of the city outside.

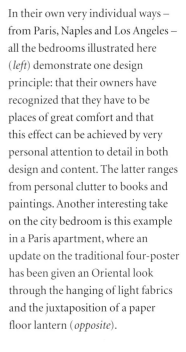

In their own very individual ways – from Paris, Naples and Los Angeles – all the bedrooms illustrated here (*left*) demonstrate one design principle: that their owners have recognized that they have to be places of great comfort and that this effect can be achieved by very personal attention to detail in both design and content. The latter ranges from personal clutter to books and paintings. Another interesting take on the city bedroom is this example in a Paris apartment, where an update on the traditional four-poster has been given an Oriental look through the hanging of light fabrics and the juxtaposition of a paper floor lantern (*opposite*).

The clean, classical lines of an old London townhouse are reflected in the simplicity of this bedroom's décor. A few simple decorative objects, reflecting the owner's interest in rustic antiques, complement exposed original floorboards and white-painted fireplace, used as display surfaces.

A taste for the baroque informs the choice of objects in this Paris bedroom. The whole arrangement, however, is set off by the exposed parquet floor. In contrast to the traditional furniture, the bed is low-level modern.

The art of stylish simplicity is common to the design of these two city bedrooms – in New York (*left above*) and in Paris (*left below*). There is a sense here of limited space being used as efficiently as possible; note especially the grille housing the heating elements in the Manhattan apartment and the shelving/cupboard unit in the Parisian example. Each bed is placed centrally in the room and below the window.

The simple lines and modulated colour schemes of modernist bedrooms can be both balanced and enhanced by the introduction of softer, more voluminous forms into the decorative scheme. These two bedrooms (*right above* and *below*) have the rigour of contemporary minimalism, yet both of them are made more inviting by the introduction of 'soft' furniture: a massive duvet; a set of outsize cushions. Treating one wall in black or grey unifies the space and reduces visual clutter.

City buildings often yield
unconventional and unusual spaces;
this loft-type area (*above*), for
instance, makes an interesting
departure from the conventional
idea of the bedroom.

Less spartan, but nonetheless spatially adventurous, is this arrangement (*above*), whereby the angle of the bed offers the opportunity for interesting views through the window.

These two bedrooms demonstrate different ways of introducing comfort into the city apartment. Both obviously go well beyond the strictly utilitarian in terms of bedroom use: the one (*left above*) through the intelligent use of bespoke furniture (the bed unit) in combination with other, free-standing elements; the other (*left below*) by a highly individual interpretation of traditional fabrics and furnishings, including an oversized easy chair.

These two bedrooms (*right above* and *below*) are clearly in city apartments spacious enough to allow considerable freedom in decoration. In both cases, one central fixture – the fireplace – has been made a focal point by its use as a display surface and the feature toward which the bed is directed.

One entirely understandable
reaction to the public demands of
urban life is to make the private
rooms of any city house or
apartment – bedrooms and studies,
say – repositories of very personal
taste and history.

 In these two highly individual
arrangements (*above* and *opposite*),
small collections of personal objects
and possessions underline the
entirely unique – and very private –
nature of these rooms.

In a city environment often characterized by strictly utilitarian concerns, there can be a certain relief in the use of traditional and well-tried fixtures in townhouse or apartment. All these bathrooms (*above* and *opposite*) eschew the built-in and bespoke in favour of old-fashioned tub baths of various kinds. An occasional decorative touch – a Warhol print or wall-clock – lends another point of interest to spaces which already invite one to linger.

Rooms sometimes derive their interest not from additional decorative elements, but from cultural references in their basic construction; in this Parisian case (*left above*), bevelled wall tiles are oddly reminiscent of those used in the city's Métro. A different angle (*left below*) on the bathroom illustrated on p.123 shows decorative details standing out against the predominant white. An antique twin basin predates and anticipates the contemporary trend for such features.

Utterly and uncompromisingly urban is this New York loft bathroom (*right above*), where the dominant decorative features are the inherited textures of the stripped brickwork and the distressed tin bath-tub. Hanging robes and folded towels add a softening touch. In contrast, this highly tailored bathroom in a Parisian apartment (*right below*) is panelled in a way oddly suggestive of a ship's cabin.

Another response to the demands of the city, above all where space is scarce and at a premium, is the all-in, built-in look. In these two examples – one in Brussels (*above left*) and one in Paris (*above right*) – an overall monochromatic look is enlivened either by small decorative touches, such as a vase of flowers, or by eccentric tilework. The fully integrated city bathroom is stylishly exemplified in a hotel in Mexico City (*opposite*).

The integrated bathroom certainly does not have to be dull; both these installations in loft-type spaces in Paris (*opposite* and *right*) exude decorative excitement, partly through innovative tilework and partly through the configuration of the main elements: baths and washbasins. One unusual addition (*right*) is an Alvar Aalto bentwood chair, originally designed in the nineteen-thirties. Both open on to a staircase.

All the bathrooms illustrated here, from London, Paris and Los Angeles, demonstrate a variety of design options (*these pages*). They are also attractive and exciting spaces, reflecting the bathroom's contemporary status as a place of serious design focus. In all cases, the quality of materials and the stylish fittings make these spaces intrinsically enjoyable. Again, a folded towel, wall photograph, or ornamental objects set off hard surfaces of zinc, stainless steel or white ceramic.

Though certainly not grand in scale, four city bathrooms of traditional design (*these pages*) have been made interesting by their owners' preferences in personal decoration and display. The sculptural qualities of the vintage fittings are much enhanced by – sometimes unlikely and unexpected – objects, light fittings and mirrors.

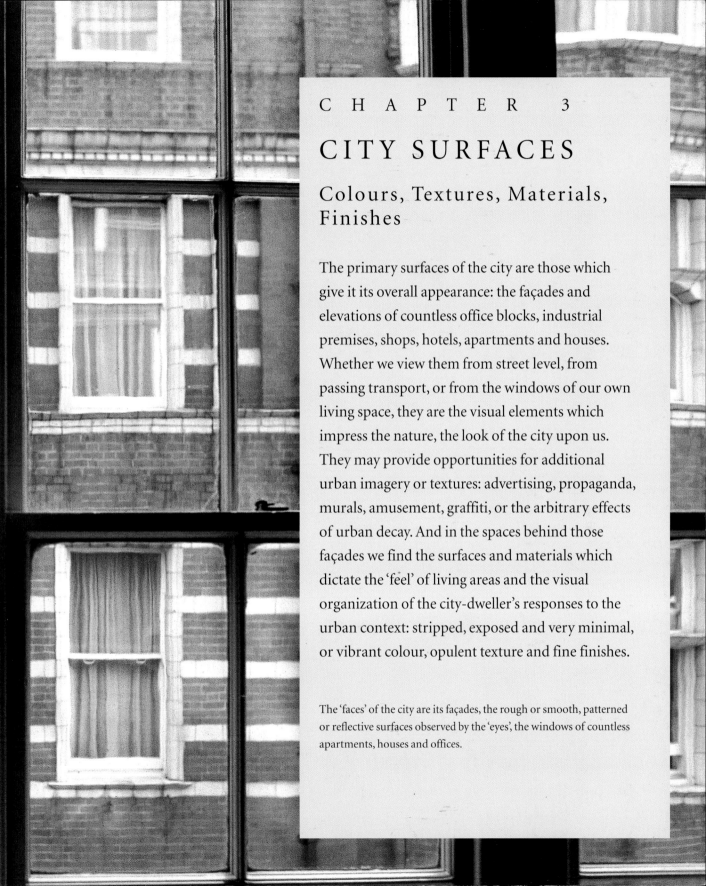

CHAPTER 3

CITY SURFACES

Colours, Textures, Materials, Finishes

The primary surfaces of the city are those which give it its overall appearance: the façades and elevations of countless office blocks, industrial premises, shops, hotels, apartments and houses. Whether we view them from street level, from passing transport, or from the windows of our own living space, they are the visual elements which impress the nature, the look of the city upon us. They may provide opportunities for additional urban imagery or textures: advertising, propaganda, murals, amusement, graffiti, or the arbitrary effects of urban decay. And in the spaces behind those façades we find the surfaces and materials which dictate the 'feel' of living areas and the visual organization of the city-dweller's responses to the urban context: stripped, exposed and very minimal, or vibrant colour, opulent texture and fine finishes.

The 'faces' of the city are its façades, the rough or smooth, patterned or reflective surfaces observed by the 'eyes', the windows of countless apartments, houses and offices.

Different cities, individual appearances: cast-iron balconies on a traditional Paris apartment block (*left above*); restoration work in Brussels (*left below*); experimental modernism in Paris (*opposite above*); the hard face of downtown Manhattan, with its iconic fire-escapes (*opposite below*).

Overleaf

The city surface outside has offered boundless opportunities for every kind of mural art, from advertising, propaganda, icon worship, *trompe-l'œil*, and the latest layer of graffiti. And, occasionally, it provides a setting for sheer whimsy, as in this apartment block elevation in San Francisco (*p.139*).

Patterns and textures on the external surfaces of the city range happily from the accidental to the deliberate, with many stages between: urban decay and the patina of the past in New York (*above left*); visual jokes in Barcelona (*above right*); formal *treillage* in Paris (*opposite left*); and accidental shadow patterns cast by wooden scaffolding in Bombay (*opposite right*).

The city within promises equally interesting textures and finishes. The fascination of old, untreated wall surfaces and their seemingly random patterns is part of a whole new way of looking at 'finish'. In this Rome apartment (*above left*) the 'rough' wall contrasts strikingly with the smoothness of the floor.

In an old London townhouse (*above right*), the owners have opted to recreate what was probably the original colour scheme for the wall as a background to a seemingly haphazard arrangement of paintings and prints.

A converted railway engine shed in Argenteuil is now home to a group of artists. In this apartment (*above left*), the wall and floor surfaces have been left in more or less their original state as a fitting background to an eclectic collection of industrial parts and 'primitive' furniture.

Again, this Marseilles loft (*above right*) has roughly treated timber-plank walls, providing background and contrast to an assembly of organic modern furniture, notably Eero Saarinen's elegant 'Tulip' chair of 1955–56.

The wall treatments illustrated here typify two distinct variations on living in the city. One seems to go with the utilitarian, practical nature of the city in its simplicity and minimalism, rationalizing limited space (*above right* and *opposite left*). The other seems to distance itself from the values of the sometimes harsh environment outside in seeking to emphasize comfort and the traditionally decorative (*above left* and *opposite right*). The minimalist examples include a wall composed partly of zinc panels, on which 'fridge magnets are used to display ad hoc graphics, and a wall treatment using panels, in which the contrasting grain directions are used to create a patchwork effect.

Patchwork is used more traditionally in the screen-printed graphics of this bedroom (*opposite right*).

The owners of three of these apartments in Paris and Brussels (*these pages*) have been fortunate enough to find that many of the original, nineteenth-century features remain intact, including tiled floors. All the surfaces illustrated here are possessed of positive visual interest and certainly require no other form of covering; they all make a very emphatic decorative statement and seem remarkably at home with all kinds of furniture, traditional or modern. One example (*above right*), however, is modern but paved with traditional tiling; this has been extended a short way up the wall to make the room look bigger.

Wood inlay (*left*) makes this floor in a Paris apartment into a dominant decorative device in a space which is already crammed with objects and ornaments. A plain floor (*right*) may also play an important role in the design of a space, throwing into relief the sculptural qualities of the furniture, including a classic Eames chair in birch-faced plywood, dating from 1945, and a wheeled cabinet reminiscent of those used in medical and dental practices.

The owners of this small East End London townhouse (*opposite*) have opted for a look which allows the inherited textures of the building's construction to show through in the form of original, untreated floorboards and whitewashed walls. An eclectic collection of classic modern furniture and rustic utensils completes a highly individual environment. In contrast, the interiors of this Paris apartment (*right*) have been given a fashionably minimalist treatment, dominated by the herring-bone pattern of the painted floor.

Opulence in the city – these two apartments (*left* and *opposite*), in Paris and New York respectively, demonstrate other options in creating interesting living spaces in the heart of major conurbations. The keynotes here are exuberant pattern and rich texture.

Overleaf
A simple, polished wood floor in a Los Angeles house has been left uncovered and uncluttered, the better to display the modernist furniture and the owner's art collection (*p.154*). How different is the floor treatment in this Paris apartment (*p.155* and *p.157*), where brilliantly coloured mats of diverse origin concentrate the eye on what lies underfoot. In moving pattern from the wall and curtains, the designer rug has become an area for interesting and inventive creative solutions – ideal for city apartments, large and small.

In tiny loft-style apartments, unlikely elements may become decorative features (*left*). Thus, a staircase to a loft sleeping gallery in this attic flat has been wittily embellished to make it an important factor in the overall definition of the room.

Twisting and turning from one level to another, this skeletal staircase (*right*) brings another interesting visual element to an apartment, without blocking light from the vast window wall.

Again, loft-type spaces which have come to typify a certain kind of city living (*left* and *opposite*); in these cases, however, the conversions have followed a tough industrial style, notably in the staircases, that contribute a robust element to the interior architecture.

Stairs and staircases can be made into central features of houses and apartments either because they are sculpturally interesting or because they provide spaces for display – of paintings or art objects, say – or storage. A particularly ingenious example of the latter is this Paris loft unit (*opposite*), which also provides important shelf space in a restricted environment. Other examples, from London, Naples, Paris, and London again (*right*) are in themselves interesting forms that are sometimes part of the original building and sometimes new, simplified versions.

If a staircase occupies a central enough position in a house or apartment, its form will clearly have a direct influence on the 'feel' of a place. Curving or spiral staircases (*these pages*), for instance, have a particularly strong presence in that they are very often intrinsically sculptural shapes in themselves and, by their very forms, create other interesting spaces, which they conceal or reveal in mounting or descending.

Managing space is an essential adjunct to successful living in the city. In these two Parisian examples (*above* and *opposite*) staircase and gallery have been used to create what are effectively two spaces out of one.

The first uses a straightforward 'ladder' stairway to a cantilevered loft gallery; the second neatly turns round the back of an adobe-style fireplace to lead up to a kitchen.

CITY DETAIL

Display, Storage, Objects, Art

The exteriors of the city have their own embellishments in architectural detail, in statuary, in a multitude of materials. In the city interior, too, it is the finishing touches which make the living spaces individual and unique in contrast to much that is uniform in the daily routines of the workplace. Personal bits and pieces, collections and possessions, family photographs and valued images, formally displayed in cabinets or on tables, or randomly distributed on open shelving, can make the plainest, four-square room into a place of wit, charm and refuge. Features, such as fireplaces, can provide points of focus for decoration and display, and even kitchens and their units, because they are usually so full of interesting shapes and objects, present marvellous opportunities for adding personality. And let us not forget the key role the florist plays in the city, providing the displays which, in colour, form and texture, bring a sense of refreshment and renewal to lives under pressure.

Façades and roofs, the exterior detail of the city, much photographed by Gilles de Chabaneix; Prague, shown here, exercised a particular fascination for him.

Books bring variety and interest to any room – in fact, they help to furnish it, especially when bookcases are constructed in unexpected places; these elegant examples, for instance, were conceived as door surrounds in a Paris apartment (*left*). A personal library, glimpsed through a wall aperture, with a sliding screen of Japanese inspiration, looks especially capacious (*opposite*).

The arrangement of books on the shelves in this formal study is an important decorative detail (*left*). They give a sense of order to the room, amplifying the effect of the imposing bookcase.

Although the bookcases in this New York apartment are actually built into the wall, their strong, simple lines create the illusion that they are free-standing. The contents of the shelves are engagingly eclectic, with ornaments and front-on display breaking up the arrangement of books (*right*).

This modernist loft-like space (*above* and *right*) manages to make a decorative virtue out of the open-shelf storage of files and documents, as well as books. In this environment every element makes a strong impression, notably the chair.

These rooms in city apartments (*left above* and *below*) really are dominated by books, giving them an overwhelmingly study/library feel.

In these bookish environments, in Paris (*right above*) and in Naples (*right below*), a real feeling of comfort and a regard for the good things of life come through the atmosphere of learning.

This intriguing capped or roofed storage unit/bookcase (*left*), the work of a distinguished Parisian furniture designer, is clearly an article of furniture with great versatility. The finish, using chestnut dowels, is characteristic of this designer's work. Another highly individual storage unit is this arrangement of shelves and panels in a Rome apartment (*opposite*); the flat surfaces and colours are strongly suggestive of a Mondrian painting.

Storage units have a supremely important role to play in the detailed organization of city spaces. And they can in themselves be important articles of furniture in any overall design, either because of their appearance or because they permit the display of other objects, such as crockery, glassware or even works of art. The examples illustrated here range from an antique cabinet in a London townhouse bathroom (*above left*) to a recycled shop unit in a Paris apartment (*above right*), open factory shelving for display (*opposite left*), and a metal drawer unit (*opposite right*), both in the same Paris apartment.

Two more examples – very different – of storage units occupying a dominant position in a room setting; this open-fronted cabinet (*left*) makes an especially strong effect through display (stones, shells, stuffed birds and animals and personal memorabilia), almost acting as a contemporary 'cabinet of curiosities', one of those collections of *naturalia* which so delighted the gentlemen-scholars of the seventeenth and eighteenth centuries. Very different is the effect of an uncompromising, industrial unit (*opposite*), made even more striking by its juxtaposition with elaborate traditional table lighting and wall sconces.

Table-top displays, just as arrangements in open cabinets or on shelves, can act as points of decorative focus, and also provide opportunities to make the most of personal possessions. All the 'shrines' illustrated here are characterized by a high degree of wit and inventiveness: an elegant floral display on a 'stork-leg' table (*above left*); a bold array of ceramics on an especially elaborate Louis-Quinze table (*above right*); an eclectic gathering of objects, extended to floor level by the two glass cloches (*opposite left*); and a neat collection of 'fifties vases (*opposite right*).

Behind the Victorian façade of a London house lies this cool, minimalist interior (*left*), partly Scandinavian and partly Oriental in inspiration. Broad boards of Oregon pine set the orderly lines of the whole ensemble at floor level. All the decorative elements of the original nineteenth-century interior have been suppressed. The removal of walls has created a set of interlocking spaces. Vestiges of the original room plan remain in the form of open fireplaces, but these have been simplified to their bare, functional essentials. Clutter is kept to an absolute minimum; even the side cushions look more symbolic than utilitarian.

One of the loft apartments created out of a disused engine shed in Argenteuil (*opposite*) reflects the semi-industrial nature of the building in its no-nonsense downlighting lamps and the massive flue casting.

The fireplace still survives as an important decorative feature in many city homes. Its traditional position in any room makes it the automatic focal point for the display of ornamental objects and art: the mantelpiece can accommodate all kinds of arrangements and clutter, while the chimney-breast is the obvious place to hang an important picture or large mirror. On either side of the fireplace the recesses created by its projecting form can be utilized easily for further wall display or for fitting bookcases and cabinets. The examples illustrated here range through burnished metal (*above left*), decorative tilework (*above right*), sculpted marble (*opposite left*), to carved wood (*opposite right*). Firedogs and other standing objects add to the overall decorative effect.

These two fireplaces (*opposite* and *right*) are features in the same Paris apartment – both pieces of decorative whimsy: the one purely conceptual, the other effectively a changing tableau of inscriptions, drawings and graphics.

Concentrated arrangements and displays of statuary and other three-dimensional objects look especially effective in the monochromatic setting of a Parisian apartment (*left* and *opposite*). The owners have deliberately reduced other decorative elements to the minimum to allow their collection of 'primitive' art to make a truly dramatic statement.

A working desk and its associated collection of objects often forms its own centre of activity as well as being an interesting focal point within a room, a sort of alternative to the main seating areas. Such an arrangement can be especially effective if the desk is also used as a setting for a still-life of unusual objects or small works of art, as in these varied examples: office style (*above left*); roll-top (*above right*); bureau (*opposite left*); and slide-out writing desk (*opposite right*).

Five examples of a more modernist take on the idea of small yet visually exciting work-stations in city apartments; these examples are drawn from Paris, Rome and Naples (*left*). Furniture in the style of Carlo Bugatti gives this Parisian corner a sculptural as well as functional air (*opposite*).

A small table by a window (*left*) can often create a pleasant space in which to read or work. Arrangements like these are especially important in small city apartments, where space is at a premium.

Such arrangements of easily movable pieces (*right*) can double as a reading area and as a pleasant spot for a solo supper.

Just as table tops may be brought to life by being covered with contrasting forms and materials, so walls are also enlivened by personal collections of paintings and other forms of art and objects, sometimes haphazardly and arbitrarily positioned to engaging effect: a collection of 'political' photographs above a carved day-bed in an Istanbul house (*above left*); urban planning charts, bringing the city inside to a Rome apartment (*above right*); books, paintings and a 'Tizio' lamp in a Parisian bedroom (*opposite left*); and children's images and artefacts in a Mexican household (*opposite right*).

An ingenious way of decorating a
city room is to make it a kind of
memory montage or scrapbook,
filling space with the images of
personal history and taste. The walls
of this Paris apartment (*above*) are
covered with photographs of the
owner's family and friends and other
valued portraits, together with
shelves of disparate objects of

personal significance. The theme of
intensely personal decoration can
take many turns (*opposite*): this
amazing collection of postcards of
rocks and boulders, for instance,
coupled with table clutter of books,
photographs and objects.

Four simple – and inexpensive – ways of making corners of city spaces both eye-catchingly decorative and personally significant at the same time (*these pages*); valued objects and images combine in a simple wall arrangement; family photographs combine with home-painted objects; panels of polaroids make a tableau of family history; a collection of antique frames makes an original and sculptural wall embellishment.

Framed images make the simplest city loft sparkle with interest (*left above* and *below*), here arranged haphazardly in keeping with the informal nature of these spaces. Also simple in arrangement but more formal are these rows of icons in a Palermo house (*opposite*).

Floral display is one immediately gratifying way of bringing colour, form and texture into any city space, especially when it is combined with other objects or images to create a variety of vignettes (*right*). With it, too, comes a sense of nature, much needed in intense urban environments. Even a single or double orchid (*opposite*) can illuminate any corner of a room; its sculptural and durable presence makes it almost a cliché in any decorative scheme for a city apartment.

Four examples of the colour and form of a floral display combining happily with the shapes, finishes and position of their holders and surrounding objects and furniture (*these pages*); careful placing against window, wall, or in relation to paintings can also serve to enhance the effect of the blooms within the whole room setting.

Although photographed in Paris, there is a distinctly Japanese look about these two minimalist table-top arrangements (*left* and *opposite*), both in the sculptural forms of the holders and the spareness of their distribution on the tables. Yet it is often such telling details that make the strongest decorative point in any room, through their form and the ingenuity and wit applied to their arrangement.

The curvilinearity of a Venini glass vase seems to relate to both the angle of the floral display and the subject of the image on the wall (*left*) in this arrangement above a shelf of antiquarian books. Curvilinear, too, is this collection of *fin-de-siècle* objects (*opposite*), finding a perfect accompaniment in an exuberant arrangement of rose varieties.

Sometimes the most unlikely places within a room setting can provide opportunities for the additions of details in witty and inventive ways, like the hanging of a striking pendant from a curtain rail in a Paris room (*left*). In another Paris flat a sumptuous tie-back (*opposite*) shows the decorative impulses of the owners extended to the minutiae of elegant living.

These two interiors, one in Paris (*above*) and one in Naples (*opposite*) exude a concern for elegant living in their attention to detail, notably in the simple, tidy groups of furniture. In both cases, curtains of an almost sculptural quality help to soften and humanize the room setting, notably in the Paris apartment, where they provide the backdrop to the brilliant colours of a Rietveld chair.

On the inside of the city looking out, windows play a major role in any room, either to make as much use of available light as possible or to preserve privacy by means of curtains and blinds which may themselves become important decorative elements. In all these cases, the blinds – and frosted glass (*opposite right*) – are used to filter light; in one ingenious San Francisco example, the blind is actually drawn up from the foot of the window (*above right*), thus protecting privacy, but also allowing in the light filtering through the foliage outside.

This modernist house in Marseilles is a veritable gallery of modern classics, including the iconic 'Butterfly' chair (*above*), originally designed in 1938, chairs and sofa by Le Corbusier, chair and ottoman by Eames, and lamp by Gae Aulenti. But one striking feature is the use of camouflage netting to create an effect of dappled shade within the long gallery (*right*).

Around the swimming pool of the
house (*preceding pages*) the military-
style netting creates a dramatic
enclosure, softening and sculptural
at the same time (*above* and *right*).

CHAPTER 5

CITY LIFE

Streets, Squares, Food Markets, Flea Markets

Among the signature photography of Gilles de Chabaneix is a series of 'overviews' of many of the major cities around the world – powerful evocations of the sheer complexity and monumentality of great urban communities. He was also fascinated by the city community at large, that vibrant life of the street and square, bars, restaurants – the wider network of urban styles, relationships, endeavours and cultures. He saw and sympathetically reported street life, where the city culture is expressed in conversations, eating and drinking on café terraces, and people simply going about their business along the thoroughfares and in the markets of their neighbourhoods. Markets, especially, feature extensively in the pages which follow: the colours, scent and vitality of the food market, bringing the fresh and natural into the city; and the flea market, which might act as a metaphor for the city's gift of recycling and renewal.

Oldest of the great French cities, Marseilles' bustling and vibrant character is aptly expressed in this jumble of façades and roofs stacked up on the city's hilly site above its port.

Cities have their own identities,
shapes and profiles, dictated by
history, tradition and climate, and
nowhere better observed than from
their rooftops: snowfall in Quebec
(*above left*); old-world charm in
Porto (*above right*); the famous *toits*
of Paris (*opposite left*); middle
European order in Prague
(*opposite right*).

Overleaf left
The many forms of street life: in
Marrakech, Cairo, New York,
Moscow, London and Paris;
More London Place – a pedestrian
precinct near Tower Bridge, beside
the river Thames (*overleaf right*).

227

The figurative imagery of the city, either in the form of freestanding statuary or as embellishments to buildings, often passes unnoticed, absorbed into the masses of masonry around or placed where it escapes the attention of the incurious passerby. It would be difficult, however, to ignore these powerful figures (*above left* and *right*) on Saarinen's Helsinki railway station, and on an Amsterdam bridge respectively. Other faces of a city look out from a window of a New York specialist in architectural salvage – a kind of recycling of the artefacts of a great city (*opposite*).

Giant atlantes support the massive entablature of one of St. Petersburg's magnificent buildings (*left*).

Other cities, other faces: a *fin-de-siècle* maiden displays her charms in Barcelona (*above left*); a complex baroque grouping embellishes a corner of old Vienna (*above right*).

Within the heavily built-up city squares and parks provide a pause, a moment for reflection, amidst the hectic life and movement of the main thoroughfares. They also bring the natural world right into the centre of the man-made. London, of all the great cities, benefits from a series of large, elegant squares (*left*) and landscaped parks (*above*).

The vitality of a city depends very much on the quality of its public life, on peaceful gatherings and conversation. All great cultures have been notable for their quality of public exchange – the ways in which they have been 'urbane'. Squares and terraces provide focal points for the community, from Los Angeles (*left above*), to a small town in Poland (*left below*).

Summer sun brings out the lunch-time crowds in London's Soho (*right above*). In Tokyo, the coming of the cherry blossom is an occasion for public celebration (*right below*).

The presence of large numbers of pedestrians in streets, squares, precincts and markets enlivens the city and reinforces its sense of community. A vigorous outside lifestyle is naturally more pronounced in places which enjoy benevolent climates: Barcelona, Athens, London and Havana (*these pages*). And what happens naturally and spontaneously in such cities is now often supported by local legislation in the Western world in the creation of pedestrianized areas.

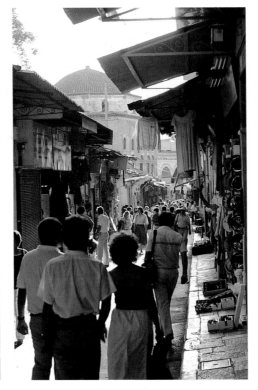

Along the city streets lie some of the most important elements of the urban life: bars, restaurants, cafés, shops and markets. These are the centres of exchange, of food and drink, money and conversation: on a café terrace in Brussels (*left above*), and in a New York flea market, a veritable treasure trove of bric-à-brac of all kinds (*left below*).

The modern city also has a longing for the fresh and natural in the midst of so much that is contrived and manufactured. One response to this trend has been the growth of farmers' markets held – usually weekly – in large conurbations, as here in New York (*right above*). Another aspect of the same impulse has been the rise of the flower market, such as this one in London's Chelsea (*right below*).

Exterior display is a vital element in the visual life of any city. Neighbourhood vendors and markets – here in Bombay (*left*) and in Naples (*opposite*) – act as focal points for local communities and provide splashes of colour in the city streets. They humanize the city, too, providing opportunities for exchange and gossip and close contact with the good things of the natural world; they are also a source of income for enterprising small traders.

This amazing image of packaging in the fish market of Tokyo (*left above*) reminds us of how important a part visual imagery plays in the life of a great city; in markets, especially, the urban feel-good factor is immensely increased by displays of abundance. Similarly, an open-fronted store, again in Tokyo (*left below*), crammed with all kinds of utensils, has a heart-warming effect, to be valued in an age of blandness and uniformity promoted by the retailing chains.

The market is rich in colour, texture, form and pattern, making its effect by the profusion of its display, as in this Tangiers stall (*right above*). It is also brought to life by the presence of people enjoying the processes of exchange, a world of buyers and sellers meeting with an immediacy impossible in more formal commercial settings: a farmers' market in New York (*right below*).

Another important city institution is the fixed market, the market-hall, a world away from the open market – here in Budapest (*above left*) and in Barcelona (*above right*). These are fixed structures, with stable groups of vendors occupying the same sites and enjoying regular custom.

In contrast, the open market, like this one in Guatemala (*opposite*), is an impromptu social event, an unplanned crowd visiting a colourful repository of everything. It is an opportunity for small farmers and country folk to get together and, most importantly, earn a living.

Flea markets are barometers of changing times and tastes in the city: yesterday's cast-offs are today's 'antiques'. The markets themselves change, too, sometimes just in direction, or even going into decline; they also respond to other urban phenomena, such as mass tourism. They do remain, however, places and scenes of interest and vitality in every major city: Brussels (*above left*); London (*above right*); Barcelona (*opposite left*); Vienna (*opposite right*).

There is sometimes a sense of pathos aroused by the displays on the margins of city markets which may act as a kind of metaphor for the complexity of this thing we call the modern city (*above*) – a sense of so many people struggling to make sense of urban life, sometimes with a trace of the absurd, as in this display of second-hand shoes (*opposite*).

The true city, though, renews itself, even after the most terrible tragedies, just as the market will reopen the next day and continue on into the future (*overleaf*).

Page numbers in *italic* refer to illustrations

Aalto, Alvar *129*
Amsterdam *27, 61, 230*
apartments 8, 11, 17, 23, *24–25, 36–37,* 38, *46–47, 50–53, 56–57, 64–65, 75, 76, 78–79, 89, 94, 104, 105, 107, 111, 125,* 135, *136, 142, 146, 148, 151, 155, 157, 168, 171, 174, 177–79, 185, 188–91, 198, 200,* 215
Argenteuil *143, 185*
Athens *238*
Aulenti, Gae *221*

balconies 10, *24,* 60
Barcelona 28, *140, 233, 238, 246, 249*
bars 8, 11
bathrooms 59, *122–33*
bedrooms *108–21*
blinds 31, *62–63, 218–19; see also* curtains
Bombay 26, *141, 242*
books/bookcases *56–57, 98–99, 168–77,* 186, *212*
Brussels 22, 26, *126, 136, 146, 240, 248*
Budapest *246*
Bugatti, Carlo 194

cabinets *149,* 167, *178, 180,* 186; filing *40*
cafés 8, 11, *240*
Cairo *228*
cast iron *60, 136*
ceramics *182*
chairs *22–23, 32–37, 41–45, 48–49, 51–57, 66–67, 69, 70–72, 74, 76, 88–107, 110, 112–13, 115–21, 123, 142–50, 152–53, 155–56, 159–60, 164, 170–75, 177–78, 180–81, 183–84, 188–89, 191, 194–99,*

203, 208–9, 216–17; Alvar Aalto bentwood *129;* 'Barcelona' *21;* 'Butterfly' *220, 223;* Eames *149;* Le Corbusier *220;* Rietveld *216;* 'Tulip' *143*
collections 42, 167, *180; see also* display
conservatories *101*
conversions 8, 17, *34–35*
cookers 76
courtyards 10
crockery *80–81,* 84, 178
cupboards 88
curtains *30, 33, 214–17; see also* blinds
cushions 23, *44–45, 54–57, 184, 196*

desks/work-stations *192–97*
dining areas *36–37, 66–67, 69, 70–71,* 88–97, *92, 95, 100, 102–3*
display 42, *70–71, 75, 78–84, 132–33, 160, 167, 171,* 178, *180, 182, 186–87, 190–91, 200–5;* exterior *242–43, 244–45;* floral 167, *182, 206–13; see also* collections
Eames *220*
Empire style *52–53*

façades *26–29,* 59, *134–35, 224–25*
'fifties style *48–49, 183*
fireplaces 112, *119,* 165, 167, *184–90*
floors 43, *44–45,* 88, 112, *143, 149;* painted *151;* parquet *113;* tiled *146–47;* wood *38, 150, 154, 184;* wood inlay *148*
floral display *see* display
furniture: Art Deco *98–99;* classic modern *151;* modernist *154;* 'primitive' *143;* rustic *56–57*

galleries 8, *164;* sleeping *156*
gardens 17, 30

glass *62–63,* 178, *219;* cloches *183*
Guatemala *247*

Havana *239*
Helsinki *230*
High-Tech style 87, 95
Hong Kong *14–15*
houses 17, *74,* 88, *96,* 106, 135, *184, 205;* townhouses 11, *60–61, 74,* 112, *142, 150, 178*

icons *205*
industrial premises 8, 35, 39, 135, *185*
Istanbul *28, 31, 84, 198*

Japanese artefacts/style *40, 106–7, 210–11*

kitchens *36–37,* 59, *62–68, 70–87,* 95, 97, *165,* 167; *see also* dining areas
Kyoto 10, *106*

lamps/lighting 23, *34–35, 40, 51–57, 70–71, 82–83, 89–95, 100–1, 103–5, 108–10, 113, 115–21, 133, 142, 147, 149, 152, 155, 175, 177, 179, 181, 185, 189, 192–93, 196, 203, 204, 216–17;* Gae Aulenti *221;* paper *40, 111, 171;* 'Tizio' *64, 199*
Le Corbusier *221*
lofts 8, *22, 39–41, 86–90,* 116, *125, 128, 129, 143, 156, 158–59, 160, 164, 172, 185*
London 8, 17, *28, 31,* 59, *74,* 112, *130, 131, 142, 150, 161, 178,* 228, *234–35, 238, 248;* Chelsea *241;* More London Place *229;* Soho *237*
Los Angeles 8, 10, 17, *18–19, 31, 48–49,* 59, *72–73, 82, 91, 96, 108, 110, 154, 236*

marble *78–79, 187*

markets 11, *225, 238, 241–43, 245, 246, 247, 250–53*; farmers' *245*; fish *244*; flea 11, *225, 240, 248–49*; flower *241*

Marrakech *228*

Marseilles *68–69,143, 220–22, 224–25*

mats *155*

Mexico *199*

Mexico City *127*

Mies van der Rohe, Ludwig *20*

Milan *76, 78–79*

minimalism 59, 88, *115, 144, 184, 210–11*

mirrors *50–51, 94, 168, 186–87*

modernism *86–87, 92, 115, 137, 172, 220–21*

Mondrian, Piet *177*

More London Place *229*

Moscow *228*

murals 135, *138–39*

Naples *31, 97, 110, 161, 175, 194, 217, 243*

netting *220–23*

New England country style *56–57*

New York 8, 17, *28, 34, 38, 56–57, 85, 86, 87, 91, 114, 125, 140, 153, 171, 228, 231, 240, 241, 245*; Manhattan *12–13, 16–17, 114, 137*

paintings/pictures 23, *34–35, 44–45, 48–49, 52–53, 94–95, 104, 109–10, 113, 115, 118–19, 130, 142, 149, 162, 164, 168, 174, 186–87, 192–99, 204, 207–9, 216*

Palermo *205*

Paris 8, 10, 17, *20, 21, 31, 35, 36–37, 39, 42, 46–47, 50–53, 62–65, 76, 77, 84, 89, 100–3, 109, 110, 111, 113–14, 124–26,* *130, 136–37, 141, 146, 148, 151–52, 155, 157, 160–61, 164–65, 168, 175, 178–79, 188–89, 190–91, 194–95, 199–200, 210, 214–16, 227–28*; Eiffel Tower *20–21*; Palais Royal *30*

parks *235*

patchwork *145*

pedestrianized areas *238–39*

photographs *46–47, 167, 198, 200–4*

Picasso, Pablo *46–47*

Poland *236*

Porto *226*

Prague 9, *58–59, 227*

'primitive' art *190–91*

Quebec *226*

restaurants 8, 11

Rome *142, 177, 194, 198*

roofs/rooftops 10, *224–27*

rugs *152, 153*

Saarinen, Eero *143, 230*

Saigon *85*

San Francisco 8, *22–23, 60, 83, 89–90, 94, 139, 218*

screens *106–7, 169*

Seine, River 10

shelves *87, 178*; open *70–71, 80–82, 83,167*

shutters *31*

sinks *77–79, 83–85*

sofas *22–25, 39, 42, 44–45, 48–49, 52–57, 104, 154, 156, 171, 175, 178, 185, 198*

squares 11, *234–38*

St. Petersburg *24, 29 , 232*

stair rails *35*

staircases *128–29, 156–63*

statuary *190–91, 230–33*

storage/storage units 35, *36–37, 64, 84, 176, 178, 180–81*

studies *170*

swimming pools *222–23*

Sydney 8, *60*

tables 20, *36–37, 41–42, 44–45, 49–57, 66–67, 69–72, 74, 76, 88–107, 113, 120–21, 142–43, 146–47, 152, 164, 167, 170, 179, 181–84, 188, 190–91, 196–97, 203, 208–9, 216–17*; Louis-Quinze *182*

Tangiers *245*

terraces *236*

textiles *56–57*

'thirties style *50–51*

tiles *76, 124, 146–47, 186*

Tokyo 8, 10, *24–25, 237, 244*

townhouses 11, *60–61, 74, 112, 142, 150, 178*

treillage 141

urban imagery 135

utensils *84–85*

vases *44–45, 53, 97, 171, 193, 208–9*; 'fifties style *183*; Venini glass *212*

Venice *26*

Vienna *233, 249*

views *24–25*

villas *60*

walls/wall treatments *115, 142, 143, 144, 198–99*

warehouses 8, 39

Warhol, Andy *122*

windows *22–23, 26–29, 30–33, 208, 218*

workshops 8

ACKNOWLEDGMENTS

Designed by Stafford Cliff
Index compiled by Anna Bennett

Any copy of this book issued by the publisher as
a paperback is sold subject to the condition that
it shall not by way of trade or otherwise be lent,
resold, hired out or otherwise circulated without
the publisher's prior consent in any form of
binding or cover other than that in which it is
published and without a similar condition
including these words being imposed on a
subsequent purchaser.

First published in the United Kingdom in 2007 by
Thames & Hudson Ltd
181A High Holborn
London WC1V 7QX

www.thamesandhudson.com

The Way We Live: In the City
© 2007 Thames & Hudson Ltd, London

All photographs
© 2007 Estate of Gilles de Chabaneix

Design and layout
© 2007 Stafford Cliff

Text and captions
© 2007 Thames & Hudson Ltd, London

All Rights Reserved. No part of this publication
may be reproduced or transmitted in any form
or by any means, electronic or mechanical,
including photocopy, recording or any other
information storage and retrieval system,
without prior permission in writing from
the publisher.

British Library Cataloguing-in-Publication Data
A catalogue record for this book is available from
the British Library

ISBN 13: 978-0-500-51336-1
ISBN 10: 0-500-51336-8

Printed and bound in Singapore by CS Graphics

The photographs in *The Way We Live* series of books are
the result of many years of travelling around the world to
carry out commissions for various publications.
Very special thanks is due to Catherine de Chabaneix, for
all her help during the production of this book, and for her
ongoing commitment to Gilles' remarkable archive.
In addition, thanks to all the people who have helped to
make the realization of this project possible, including
Martine Albertin, Béatrice Amagat, Catherine Ardouin,
Françoise Ayxandri, Marion Bayle, Jean-Pascal Billaud,
Anna Bini, Marie-Claire Blanckaert, Barbara Bourgois,
Marie-France Boyer, Marianne Chedid, Alexandra
D'Arnoux, Jean Demachy, Emmanuel de Toma, Geneviève
Dortignac, Jérôme Dumoulin, Marie-Claude Dumoulin,
Lydia Fiasoli, Jean-Noel Forestier, Marie Kalt, Françoise
Labro, Anne Lefèvre, Hélène Lafforgue, Catherine Laroche,
Nathalie Leffol, Blandine Leroy, Marianne Lohse,
Véronique Méry, Chris O'Byrne, Christine Puech, José
Postic, Nello Renault, Daniel Rozensztroch, Elisabeth Selse,
Suzanne Slesin, Caroline Tiné, Francine Vormèse, Claude
Vuillermet, Suzanne Walker, Rosaria Zucconi and
Martin Bouazis.

Our thanks also go to those who allowed us access to their
houses and apartments: Jean-Marie Amat, Mea Argentieri,
Avril, Claire Basler, Bébèche, Luisa Becaria, Dominique
Bernard, Dorothée Boissier, Carole Bracq, Susie and Mark
Buell, Michel Camus, Laurence Clark, Anita Coppet and
Jean-Jacques Driewir, David Cornell, Bertile Cornet, Jane
Cumberbatch, Geneviève Cuvelier, Ricardo Dalasi, Anne
and Pierre Damour, Catherine Dénoual, Dominique and
Pierre Bénard Dépalle, Phillip Dixon, Ann Dong, Patrice
Doppelt, Philippe Duboy, Christian Duc, Jan Duclos
Maïm, Bernard Dufour, Explora Group, Flemish
Primitives, Michèle Fouks, Pierre Fuger, Massimiliano
Fuksas, Teresa Fung and Teresa Roviras, Henriette
Gaillard, Jean and Isabelle Garçon, John MacGlenaghan,
Fiora Gondolfi, Annick Goutal and Alain Meunier,
Murielle Grateau, Michel and Christine Guérard, Yves and
Michèle Halard, Hotel Le Sénéchal, Hotel Samod Haveli,
Anthony Hudson, Ann Huybens, Patrick T'Hoft, Igor and
Lili, Michèle Iodice, Paul Jacquette, Hellson, Jolie Kelter
and Michael Malcé, Amr Khalil, Dominique Kieffer,

Kiwayu Safari Village, Lawrence and William Kriegel,
Philippe Labro, Karl Lagerfeld, François Lafanour, Nad
Laroche, Rudolph Thomas Leimbacher, Philippe Lévèque
and Claude Terrijn, Marion Lesage, Lizard Island Hotel,
Luna, Catherine Margaretis, Marongiu, Mathias, Valérie
Mazerat and Bernard Ghèzy, Jean-Louis Mennesson, Ilaria
Miani, Anna Moï, Leonardo Mondadori, Jacqueline
Morabito, Christine Moussière, Paola Navone, Christine
Nicaise, Christian Neirynck, Jean Oddes, Catherine Painvin,
John Pawson, Christiane Perrochon, Phong Pfeufer,
Françoise Pialoux les Terrasses, Alberto Pinto, Stéphane
Plassier, Morgan Puett, Bob Ramirez, Riad Dar Amane, Riad
Dar Kawa, Yagura Rié, Guillaume Saalburg, Holly Salomon,
Jérôme-Abel Séguin, Jocelyne and Jean-Louis Sibuet, Siegrid
and her cousins, Valérie Solvi, Tapropane Villa, Patis and
Tito Tesoro, Richard Texier, Jérôme Tisné, Doug Tomkins,
Anna and Patrice Touron, Christian Tortu, Armand Ventilo,
Véronique Vial, Barbara de Vries, Thomas Wegner, Quentin
Wilbaux, Catherine Willis.
Thanks are also due to the following magazines for allowing
us to include photographs originally published by them:
Architectural Digest (French Edition), *Atmosphère*, *Coté Sud*,
Elle, *Elle à Table*, *Elle Décoration*, *Elle Décor Italie*, *Madame
Figaro*, *Maison Française*, *Marie Claire*, *Marie Claire Idées*,
Marie Claire Maison, *The World of Interiors*.

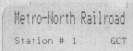

Metro-North Railroad

Station # 1   GCT

Sold Tickets   Amount
One Way Peak $12.50
One Way Peak $12.50
OW Off Peak $9.50
OW Off Peak $9.50

Total Amount $44.00

Payment: Cash $44.00

Thank You for Riding
Metro North !
TSM ID #   206
Transaction #   323614
Date / Time   09/19/03 16:43

1012 1984 09392

RABATKORT: KR. 4.50

WEST KENSINGTON

019064   UVC   UVC
07:00P NOV 14 04
ONE WAY R $1.25
177

OBLITERAR
TARIFA DE BORDO
ON BOARD TICKET

U   0543511

CityRail

Rail Clearways
Untangling our complex rail network

www.cityrail.info

for more frequent, reliable CityRail services

Return ticket valid up to 4am after day of issue

SUTHERLAND AND RTN
MASCOT   CITYRAIL
GST $1.03
10JUL06 $11.30

東京 TOKYO
18.-7.-7
130円
7338 13:08

47.-2.12
北千里 30円
6232

SPACE
RATP
GARNET
00246664 H 1609 A2

Metro
Sencillo
064870
NO DOBLAR
07/07/99
13:18

M.T.T., ADELAIDE

BLACK DIAMOND CORNER

B J G 177324